Debts your dirty little secret:

Tips and motivation to be financially free

By

Cally Finsbury

I0489980

www.callyfinsbury.somespecialpeople.com

purchase an additional copy for each person you share it with.

Printed in the United Kingdom

First Printing, 2016

Publisher code:

ANRMXON65MTOW

somespecialpeople@gmail.com

Some Special People Publishing

296 Cann Hall Road, London, E11 3NN

www.somespecialpeople.com

Also by Cally Finsbury

The Anxious Caterpillar

Cally and the Ant

Amazing Nathan No Ordinary Boy

Amazing Child

Glimpse: A peep into school life

Gifted Sammy No Ordinary Child

Disclaimer

I do not provide personal investment advice and I am not a qualified licensed investment advisor. I am an amateur investor.

All information found here, including any ideas, opinions, views, predictions, forecasts, commentaries, suggestions, or stock picks, expressed or implied herein, are for informational, entertainment or educational purposes only and should not be construed as personal investment advice. While the information provided is believed to be accurate, it may include errors or inaccuracies.

I will not and cannot be held liable for any actions you take as a result of anything you read here.

Conduct your own due diligence, or consult a licensed financial advisor or broker before making any and all investment decisions. Any investments, trades, speculations, or decisions made on the basis of any information found on this site, expressed or implied herein, are committed at your own risk, financial or otherwise.

Somespecialpeople is my personal weblog. It reflects my own views, ideas and opinions. It is not a production of my employer, nor is it affiliated with any broker/dealer or registered investment advisor.

No representations or warranties are made with respect to the accuracy or completeness of the content of this entire weblog, including any links to other sites. The links provided are maintained by their respective organizations and they are solely responsible for their content. All information presented here is provided 'as is', without warranty of any kind, expressed or implied.

From time to time I may include affiliate links and advertisements on my blog or in this book that result in my receiving a payment should a visitor click on a link or sign up to a service, as per established Internet practice. Readers are entirely responsible for any actions they take as a result of reading or clicking on links on the site, and are urged to read the small print!

Contents

Chapter 1: Introduction

Hooray! You found a partner and you should be really happy but the problem is they owe a lot of money and have debts. This book is for you if you would like some practical tips and advice about how to manage and eventually remove major debt from your daily life. If you haven't got any debts but you want to know so you can help a friend or family member this book is for you. There are sections where you can find out specific things and there are sections that give you insight into where you should find out where you can go for further advice. Good luck if you are in a new or significant relationship and you want to sort out financial worries.

My best friend told me about her problems and asked if I would help. I am going to share with you the tips and strategies I gave to her. You have a goal and now you have a plan of action to help you to achieve your goal.

Chapter 2: The dirty little secret

Relationships can come with different types of baggage but one that is loaded with debt can be very challenging. There needs to be an open and honest discussion about how much money is owed and to whom.

It can be really frightening having the conversation about your debts but it is important that before the meeting you make a comprehensive list of the debts so if words fail you there is the option to show it to your partner and they can see for themselves.

Once you are clear on how much is owned and both of you are calm, you can voice your opinions in a calm and rational way. Be prepared for looks of disappointment and disapproval if this is the first time your partner is hearing about this debt. They may be in serious shock and you must allow for this and try to remain focused on your task of informing your partner of your debts and working out a plan of action.

Now you may think why you should have to justify or defend the debts but remember if this person is to feel involved they may just be asking questions because they are shocked at how easily and quickly you accumulated the debts (or how much is owed or that you were able to keep it a secret).

You now need to look at the debts, there are different types of debts and it is important that you both understand the implications for them:

Secured debt: is supported by collateral, like a house or a vehicle

Unsecured debt: has no collateral, like credit cards or individual loans

Fixed interest rate debt: has the same interest rate for the whole timeline of the loan, like a mortgage

Variable interest rate debt: the interest rate may alter over the life of the loan, like credit cards

Fixed payment term: the loan is set to be paid off by a definite date, like a mortgage or student loan

Variable repayment period: There is no definite date by when the debt must be repaid, like credit cards

Deductible: this loan is used to better your individual situation and therefore may have tax benefits, like a mortgage or student loan

Non-deductible: a loan that has no advantage to your wellbeing. Is not used to acquire an appreciating asset or new skill, like credit cards or a personal loan

Source http://lifehacker.com/the-most-common-types-of-debt-and-how-to-tackle-them-1688461004

Now your dirty little secret is out take a deep breath and be aware that you are one step closer to solving your financial worries (always keep your goal in mind).

Chapter 3: What now? My partner has calmed down

Good news your partner has had time to think and is calm and ready to discuss your financial predicament. What you need to do now is have a look at how your financial income and expenditure develops. Now there are certain things that all adults will have to pay and there are things that will be specific to you. Use this as a guideline and a prompt to get you thinking. Depending on where you live in the World, the names of things may also vary:

Income

Wages

Salary

Working tax credit

Child tax credit

Job seeker's allowance

Income Support

Child Benefit

Other State benefit

Other income

So you have a list of possible sources of money that you may have coming in. Now it is time to examine the expenditure (what you spend your money on).

Expenditure

This just means those expenses you have regularly to just live. Once again I shall remind you that these things may be called something different but they should prompt you and guide you:

Mortgage

Second mortgage

Rent

Ground rent

Service charges

Council Tax

Buildings Insurance

Contents Insurance

Life Insurance

Endowment Policy

Gas bill

Electricity bill

Water Rates

Food

TV subscriptions

Club subscriptions

Meals

Coffee

Clothing

Entertainment

Miscellaneous other

Chapter 4: Questions you need to discuss

Am I clear how much money I have coming in?

Do I know when I get paid?

Do I know when and how I get the money I have coming in?

Do I know when my bills are due?

When you have discussed these things with your partner you should be ready for the next step.

What else should I think about?

Do I feel confident to keep going?

Do I need to talk to someone else?

Do I need a debt counsellor?

Chapter 5: Are you ready for the next step?

You have gotten over the worst of it, you have admitted you owe money and have debts. You need to remind yourself that today is today but tomorrow is tomorrow and one day in the future you will look back with pride knowing your finances are in order.

The next step involves really examining your situation. Who are you in arrears with? How should you evaluate your debts priorities? This can mean different things to different people but to me it means being aware of the negative effects of debts and arrears that can end up taking away your liberties and financially ruining your credit history.

You should notice that these are also the things that are part of your daily living with added ones that may result because you have fallen behind in your payment schedule arrears charges and late payment charges or court fees:

Mortgage arrears

Secured loan arrears

Ground rent arrears

Service charge arrears

Rent arrears

Council Tax arrears

Gas arrears

Electricity arrears

Magistrate Court Fine

Income Tax

Maintenance arrears

Other

Now you have listed them you need to consider how you have actually been managing their payment each month. I need you to be honest. If you have just been putting them in a draw or bin you need to find out how much you actually owe. I know it is really hard to do this but every step brings you that little bit closer to sorting out your financial worries. Please keep going, it really will be worth it and I know it is important to you.

Now you have done that, I need you to think carefully about anything you may have forgotten to include for instance; credit cards or store cards (you know that secret card that you use for emergencies or comfort purchases). So we are getting closer. **KEEP YOUR GOAL IN MIND.**

Chapter 6: How will I pay the money?

My friend looked at me and tears were in her eyes and she asked me: *"How will I pay the money?"*

I told her what I am telling you: where there is a will there is a way.

This chapter is the research results for ways to make additional income. If you just want to know about strategies to clear your debt rather than increasing your income you can skip this chapter and find out about letters you can write to reduce your debt and make them more manageable.

Depending on what your interests are, there are different ways to increase your income and allocate that money towards clearing your debts.

I found some ways that you can increase your income and work towards clearing those debts, these methods can be done with your partner to increase bonding in this challenging time and also to demonstrate to your partner you are willing to do additional work to clear the debts and to create a safety net for the future.

We deliberately found activities that you can do at home or where you have access to a computer or smartphone.

(Remember internet safety when using shared computers).

I will give you some suggestions and hopefully they will prompt you into action.

These examples of things all relatively easy to do. There are more details at the end of this chapter if any of the activities appeal to you.

Completing surveys

Completing questionnaires

Completing small tasks

Investigations

Making things

Creating items for sell

Selling things

Being a mystery shopper

Improving things

The list is just to prompt you and stimulate your thinking.

Don't laugh, my friend actually laughed out loud when I suggested to her to play games or do tasks. Her exact words were: "Are you serious? Games and scanning tasks are for children, I am a grown woman". My reply was slightly less than helpful but this gist was, do you want my help? If you do just listen to my suggestion and determine if it is something that will get us that step closer to being financially worry free.

So if you are smirking or thinking: is she off her trolley? I suggest to you to read on or skip to another example, the choice is yours. You are in charge every step of the way, if you don't like something or don't want to try it then don't. (Obviously when I calmed down I apologised and explained that I like to play games and I am top 10% on DX Pac Man)

Whatever your skill set, I hope you can find something that appeals to you:

FieldAgents

What is that you ask? This is an opportunity to do tasks that vary from finding out about products or finding out the price of an item. The tasks vary considerably and you may have to check or scan barcodes or qr codes.

Write music reviews

You can earn money giving your views and opinions on music.

An example of a website is Slice The Pie

Creating tasty and good value recipes

Are you good at cooking or making things on a budget? If you are or are willing to ask friends and family for their recipes you could to submit to Paypal for £5

Swagbucks

How can you make money playing games you wonder? Make money playing online games you like may provide rewards. You can make virtual money and exchange it for real money, you can complete surveys, play games and a lot more.

You can earn rewards and points by using their search engines to do your research

Just go to the swagbucks link below try it out.

http://www.swagbucks.com/register?rb=19722021&cmp=72&cxid=1200-twitter

Completing surveys or questionnaires

This may be done online and there are surveys of varying lengths, most give an estimated time so you can pick the ones to suit your timeframe.

Examples of online survey providers are:

MySurvey

Skills you can share

Join an online site like Fiverr that has a variety of options available. Even if there is just one small thing you can do, there may well be someone that needs just that skill to complete their job.

For instance you might be good a proofreading, writing product reviews, translating, singing etc.

Fiverr has several sections which also have subsections; I have listed a few so you can match your skill sets to the examples:

Graphic and Design

Cartoons

Logo designs

Illustrations

Book cover design

Photoshop editing

Flyers and posters

Invitations

Digital Marketing

Web Analytics

Domain Research

Social marketing

Local Listings

Writing and Translations

CVs and Cover letters

Research and Summary

Blog Posts

Video and Animation

Whiteboard Animation

Testimonials

Introductions

Lyrics and Music videos

Video Greetings

Music and Audio

Voice overs

Sound effects

Session musicians

Singers and Songwriters

Programming

Convert files

Web programming

Advertising

Hold your sign

Flyers and Handouts

Human Billboards

The list previously are all things you can be hired to do on services like Fiverr or Elance and there are so many more example so think about what interests you.

Mystery shopping

Please do your research and do not pay for any services.

Mystery Shoppers are specialists in the field of mystery shopping and customer satisfaction research.

http://www.mystery-shoppers.co.uk/

http://www.marketforce.com/en-gb/become-a-mystery-shopper

Craigslist

This suggestion is for anyone! Think about it! There must be something you can think of to do on Craigslist. What are your interests? What skills do you have? What things in your home do you no longer need or use? Is there a bargain shop that you know that you could purchase things and sell them on for profit?

Craigslist is one of the most visited sites online and therefore there are all kinds of opportunities. Look for free or really inexpensive items in the free section and then make the item look attractive and turn around and sell them for a profit.

Sell on eBay

The same sort of skills and questions you use for Craigslist can be applied to

Ebay. It is up to you to think what opportunities await you on Ebay.

Anyone can sell on eBay and you are likely already somewhat familiar with it. It is a terrific place to start earning extra money if you have the right product to offer.

Remember you plan to be financially worry free, so you focus on the things that will make you additional income. Do you know the 80/20 rule? Use your time carefully and give yourself a specific amount of time to search with your complete focus.

Know what you are doing and keep your search organised and then move on so that you will really concentrate on finding that bargain item to make extra money.

Do you use a computer or know how to use search engines? If the answer is yes this is another possible opportunity for you. You can be essential to someone by doing searches or being a virtual assistant. You can then be hired help or you could hire someone to do a task for you and you could gain additional income.

Product Reviews

Everyone has an opinion on something they have purchased or used. But how can you make that something that helps you to get one step closer to being financially worry free? You can write or contact anyone who makes or sells a product you use and tell them your opinion. They might send you vouchers or codes which will save you money. If you find that you really enjoy doing product reviews you could go one step further.

Establish or create your own blog or website and begin discussing products. You can contact website owners to promote your service, letting others know that you will post a review of their website on your website.

Design T-shirts

Who hasn't worn a t-shirt before? What is your favourite t-shirt? Why do you like that t-shirt? Could you design a t-shirt that other people might like?

If you love to create cool designs or you are always coming up with cool phrases then you'll be terrific at designing and selling t-shirts. Sites like CafePress offer you an easy way to market your products and there are also crowd funding sites that offer you a great way to sell your products.

Do your research to find out more about the opportunities to find out about design opportunities.

Another one is to use your skills to make templates. What kind of templates?

Create Digital Scrapbooking Templates – There are huge numbers of people that scrapbook and they pay dearly for templates they like so if you can make different kinds of templates that are easy to use, do a great job and more people will support you and you may gain a strong following and make money.

There you have it, several ways to increase or make additional income. Some of these might not be for you. But if even one appeals to you and you can raise additional income to put towards your debts and you continue to do it once you are financially worry free would that really be something to make you smile?

Chapter 7: Willpower

This book is designed to prompt and point you in the direction to gain further knowledge and understanding. Why a chapter on willpower? To provide a little taste for the people that need to have awareness or knowledge of key research on the area they are interested in. So this chapter may be skipped if you do not have to be convinced that it is possible to change a habit that you have established. In other words, just because you have always purchased a coffee and a bagel for breakfast on the way to work doesn't mean you can't change that habit and establish a new routine.

Willpower and motivation are the keys to your new future. Hence, here are some brief and concise research so you feel more confident to know it is okay if you are finding it challenging or you have had a setback. If you believe it, you can achieve your goal of being financially worry free.

The American Psychological Association in their annual survey reported that the majority of respondents believed that willpower is something that can be learned.

Research by Roy Baumeister, PhD, psychologist at Florida State University also stated that it you want to have a better chance of achieving your goal you need three components:

Establishing the motivation for change and setting clear goal.

Monitoring the behaviour towards that goal.

Exercising willpower.

Whether your goal is to reduce your lunch bill or save towards clearing your debts, willpower is a critical step to achieving the outcome you desire. (Source American Psychological

Association: What you need to know about willpower)

There has also been a vast amount of research conducted on willpower. Kathleen Vohs & Ronald Faber a professor at University of Minnesota discovered that willpower can be impacted by how frequently you have to exercise it. In other words, if you want to avoid the temptation of overspending or continuing unwanted behaviour, you will have more success if you do not have to use your willpower rapidly or in close durations. (Source American Psychological Association: What you need to know about willpower)

Princeton University doctoral applicant Dean Spears found that it can be more challenging to discipline yourself when you are in a position of financial hardship. Therefore, you must remember when shopping to make sure that you are not hungry or thirsty and ensure that you are prepared for the shopping excursion so you are not tempted to spend unnecessary money. (Source American Psychological Association: What you need to know about willpower)

The Stanford experiment

Walter Mischel's book was intriguing because it had an experiment to explore delayed gratification. Some of the participants explained and revealed that having a strategy to avoid temptation is beneficial to your success. A child is presented with a marshmallow and given a choice: Eat the marshmallow straight away, or wait and get double the marshmallows. The experiment demonstrated the strategies and effort the children show to not eat the marshmallow. Follow up studies showed correlations between those who deferred gratification and later academic success in life.

When you read through this book you will know the strategies to succeed and this will help you. My son participated in a marshmallow test and he told me his strategy was not to look at the marshmallow and focus on what he wanted to achieve which was to get double the reward.

I hope from this basic research you will know that having a goal and a plan of action makes you one step closer to being financially worry free.

Chapter 8: Staying motivated

Why have you added a chapter on staying motivated? My friend looked at me one day and said she had enough and would just go to her grave with the debt. This had a double meaning to me and I was very anxious for my friend.

I acknowledge that owing a lot of money is very distressing but it can be something that is eliminated if you stay motivated and remember what you want to achieve.

Bruce Lee said something that has stayed in my mind: "If you love life, don't waste time, for time is what life is made up of."

One of my favourite authors Charles Haanel, inspired me to have goals and what type of person you need to be. I want to know that I am whole, perfect, loving, harmonious, powerful, strong and happy. He made me realise that you need to feel good.

I know that I feel good everyday and others are starting to feel good. People often ask me why do I feel so good? I tell them about the good days and the slightly less good times and that they can feel good as well. So getting financially worry-free can be challenging but you will feel good knowing that you are working towards a goal that will make you feel so good.

Let us use our time well every day, so we fulfil our dreams, being free of financial burdens and be like me, I know that I am feeling good and those around me are feeling good also.

Thomas Edison once remarked: "Time is the only capital any human being has and the only thing he cannot afford to lose."

Good luck to us all on this wonderful journey of life, let us be the best version of ourselves and fulfil our hopes and dreams. You know one of your hopes is to be financially worry free so stay focused and know that you are one step closer.

Don't blame yourself for setbacks just smile and keep on remembering your goal.

Chapter 9: Remember to smile: it is free

My friend has persistence, so I continued to tell her what she needed to do. Yet again she was down trodden and looking glum so I reminded her of something I wanted to share with you. Something that many of us take for granted. You may owe a lot of money but you will always have something that is free and extremely powerful. Your smile.

Smiling is so powerful and it is something that we can all do. You may find yourself smiling when you think about your day or that special someone, it can happen anywhere or at any moment.

I know smiling can improve your whole mood. I have another friend who when we are in a meeting and I smile at her she just gets what I am thinking and we reflect each other's smile. When we look around the room we see others have started smiling too.

Sometimes that smile can transform into a giggle and when you are laughing and smiling it is one of the best feelings in the world. I have found some really brilliant blogs and they just make me smile and laugh as I relate to the experiences or picture the situations.

A smile from your child can make you just fall in love with your child over and over again. One of the best feelings is the smile you get when your child sees their mummy and daddy have come to collect them from school, the way your child's smile radiates makes you get butterflies.

A smile can signal forgiveness: a stern faces starts to soften and you know you are about to be forgiven. When your loved one receives that smile it lets them know you are sorry for upsetting them for having so much financial debt and owing so much money.

A smile can turn into a grin that signals that someone is going to have a very enjoyable evening and that you are so glad that someone loves you dearly.

So if you can start your day with a lovely smile. I highly recommend it! Thanks to my wonderful son who starts each day and night by putting his big cheesy smile right in my face as soon as he wakes up and before he goes to sleep. I love my children dearly and I love that a gesture like a smile can give so much hope and love.

So I suggest to you to remember the power of your smile and I hope you give and receive many.

Take care and thanks for all those wonderful blogs and people who make us smile.

So remain focused and always remember your goal to be financially worry free.

Chapter 10: Payment strategies

Here are 10 tips that you can easily do that help in different ways. The first one, for instance, helps because it will reduce your financial outgoings. It will do this because depending on which deal you get, you will get a duration when you will not have to pay for a set period or you will pay a reduced amount. Once again, I remind you that it depends on which part of the World you are in and names of things may vary.

In the UK, you could apply for a new credit card that has a 0% balance transfer rate but I am warning you do not be tempted to use this as an opportunity to gain access to further debt. Remember your goal to be financially worry free.

1. Switch to a 0% balance transfer credit card

If you're paying interest on credit card debt, think about switching your balance to a 0% balance transfer deal - the best deals currently offer up to 28 months interest-free.

Do your research and find the best deal for you.

2. Reject increases in your credit card APR

If you have credit card debt and your rate is going to be increased, you have 60 days to contact the company and let them know you do not want the rate to increase. You won't be able to use the card for further spending, but you will be able to repay anything you already owe at your old, lower rate.

Do your research and find out what is applicable to your situation.

3. Join your local credit union

Loans from credit unions are generally cheaper than loans from most other providers for smaller amounts and do not incur set-up fees, administration costs or early redemption fees.

Many credit union loans are far cheaper than other loans on the open market.

Do you have a financial group that helps people in your predicament?

Do your research and find out what is applicable to you.

4. Avoid payday loans and other forms of high cost credit

You must remember that the rate of interest you pay on a loan or debt will have a significant impact. If the rate is ridiculously high it will be very difficult to have any impact when trying to pay it off.

If you have a payday loan or a loan that is ridiculously high, do your research and find out if you can get a cheaper rate.

5. Improve your credit score

Before you apply for credit, check your credit report with Experian, Equifax and Callcredit. If there are errors on your file, or if you have a poor credit history, this may reduce your chances of acceptance when you apply for a loan, as well as increase the interest rate you'll be offered if your application is successful.

Do your research and find out how to improve your credit score and how to get a copy of your credit report.

6. Pay more than the minimum on your credit card

If you only make the minimum payment on your credit card, not only will it take you longer to repay the full balance, you may also be damaging your credit score.

Your credit report records whether you make the minimum payment or a bigger amount – if overpaid on your debts and may be beneficial to your finances. The advantages is that it will also help to clear the debt quicker but remember to clear the debts with the highest rate of interest and the debts that provide you with somewhere to live.

Do your research and find overpayment calculators so you can see how much money you can save?

7. Consolidate your debts with a personal loan

If your interest rate on your credit card is high, consider getting a personal loan which should be at a lower rate and use this to repay your credit card.

Do your research and go on comparison sites to find out about the best deals available to you. REMEMBER every application leaves a trail.

8. Get independent, free debt advice

If you can't afford the repayments on existing debt, it's better to get free, independent advice rather than getting further into financial trouble by using fee-charging debt management companies.

Find out if your government offers debt free advice

9. Get an authorised overdraft

Before you get charged overdraft fees arrange with the bank to get an overdraft.

Always try to think ahead of any situation for instance get that overdraft sorted before you need it. Avoid charges and fees because you exceed your existing overdraft limit, speak to your bank as soon as possible as they may be willing to increase your authorised overdraft. Going into unauthorised overdraft will cause a whole host of extra charges and can be even more costly than a payday loan.

Do your research to find the best deals available to you on comparison websites.

Remember applications leave a trail on your credit file.

10. Pay off debt before saving

While it's good to have a financial cushion for use in emergencies, there's little logic in having savings if you also owe money on a credit card or overdraft.

Sometimes it is better to put the main amount of your money towards clearing debts and the minor part towards an emergency fund.

Here is an example from: http://www.moneysavingexpert.com/savings/pay-off-debts

£1,000 debts on a credit card at 18%

The interest cost is: £180

£1,000 Savings in a saving account at 1.5%

The interest earned is £15

Pay off the debt with the savings and you are £165 a year better off.

Do your research and decide what to do, remember debts usually cost a lot more than savings can earn. When you are financially worry-free then it is time to save more.

Chapter 11: Use cash to help to stay in control

Seeing is believing when you actually see the physical cash, it will actually make you realise how much you are spending. There are a number of systems in place with various names but in short it is an envelope or container or wallet that should be used to allocate money to different sources. For instance, £10 could be sectioned off for lunch and once that fund is finished no more can be allocated. £10 could be allocated for transport and once that is finished no more may be allocated. So what are the implications? Once the money in that envelope is spent, there's nothing left for that allocation. If you wanted to eat out for lunch one day after this you will have to use the extra food in your fridge because there is no money left in the lunch envelope.

The reason why this method is so effective is because you remain in charge the whole time. You may still have your treats but you accept that you may have to do without for something on another occasion.

Make a list of things you need and then you can think about a budget. You may have already done this in a previous chapter (the book is designed to be read however you please).

Make a daily list, here is an example to prompt and guide you:

Breakfast

Lunch

Snacks

Drinks

Transport

Entertainment

Other

What can you purchase at the supermarket to save you money?

What can you make at home?

What can you do without?

Is there a less expensive alternative?

What else do you need to consider?

Chapter 12: How to stay more financially free

You are almost there. What now? These tips for being more financially free may help you to reduce and eventually eliminate your debts.

Things you need to think about and discuss with your partner:

How do you reduce your expenses so that there is more money to put towards the debts?

Let us examine Gas and Electric bills:

Are you on the best tariff? How do you find out? Look on your bill, check comparison sites, call and find the best rate for you.

Think about when you use your gas and electricity. When do you set the timer for the heating to turn on? Do you adjust the settings to take into consideration the weather or the time of day?

Can you get a thermostat fitted to control the temperature?

Think about when you use your appliances. Could you do you washing and drying at a less expensive time of day?

In short is there any way you can reduce your gas and electric bills?

Entertainment: do you have subscriptions to things you can reduce or eliminate? Do you need so many subscriptions?

Find out if they will do a reduced deal if not tell them you need to reduce or cancel or subscription.

Eating out: ways to save money. It is okay to go out for that special occasion but can you reduce or eliminate the frequency of eating out. Maybe order less when you go to that restaurant. Perhaps cook a meal and invite friends round or cook parts of the meal or do a potluck night with friends. Maybe you could split the cost of the meal. Let your friends know about your goal, they may pleasantly surprise you by being very supportive.

Know the warning signs or triggers that tempt you to comfort or impulse shop. Can you reduce or eliminate your impulse shopping. Can you shop at a less expensive location?

Be informed and know words that will help you towards your goal of being financially worry free. For instance, compound interest. When you owe money this increases your debt when you own money it increases your wealth. Compound interest means each month you owe the original amount and the interest until you pay it off. In other words you are paying interest on the interest.

Chapter 13: Shopping: How and when to shop

Thinking ahead and making lists is something I highly recommend. When deciding what you need, a list will ensure you think carefully and stay within a reasonable spending allowance.

Always do your best to check your cupboards, fridge or shelves before you start the shop so you are clear what you need and what treats you can afford?

Use a system like the envelope system so you only carry cash and don't spend more than you can afford or that you want to.

Credit cards and cash cards provide the opportunity to overspend so don't take them with you. Avoid temptation and leave additional sources of spending at home.

Using the calculator on your mobile phone or an actual physical calculator can help you to have a realistic idea of what you are spending and can help you to work out if something is financially beneficial to you.

When buying food, be willing to go to several locations to get the best price for different types of food.

Check the dates, sometimes stores reduce items.

Check the dates to avoid purchasing items that will be off before you are ready to use them.

Another way to save money is to plan your meals for the week so you know exactly what you need and you avoid waste.

Purchase containers and freeze bags so you can freeze leftover food but make sure it can be frozen and is appropriately cooled before refrigeration or freezing and fully defrosted and reheated before consumption.

There are cashback sites like QuidCo that have the advantage that you receive cashback when you use their site to do your shopping.

Chapter 14: Food for you to save money but still taste tasty!

What food is flexible and can help you to be financially worry free? These items will save you money because you will leave your home having had a filling and nutritious breakfast. You will have a variety of choices for your breakfast, lunch, dinner and snacks. The need to purchase things on the go should be reduced or eliminated.

Fruits

Variety of cereals

Variety of breads

Rice

Pasta

Beans

Lentils

Eggs

Variety of fish

Variety of poultry

Variety of teas and hot drinks

Coffee

Sugar

Salt

Pepper

Variety of crisps

Variety of tin foods

Variety of quick frozen food

Variety of snacks

Butter

Variety of cheeses

Variety of desserts

Do your research find out about special offers and foods that appeal to you. If you can make it or purchase it at the supermarket you could save money.

Meal ideas

What could you have for breakfast so you don't waste money on the way to work?

How about one of the followings?

Pancakes are quick and easy to make or you could buy the add milk or water packets.

French toast is a tasty breakfast treat.

Toast is quick and easy and there is the option of different toppings.

Packets of waffles or muffins are fine once in awhile as a tasty treat and should still be less expensive than purchasing from a bakery or cafe.

Croissants can be purchased frozen or fresh from most supermarkets.

What could you have for lunch so you don't waste money on the way to work or during your lunch break?

Soup: fresh or canned or just add water can be a quick and tasty inexpensive treat especially when the weather is chilly.

Salads can be made quickly and be used as a lunch meal and for your dinner. Find out about the different types of lettuce and kale which can be tasty and very good for you.

Sandwiches can be very interesting by using different types of bread and similarly different types of fillings. Use the microwave or toaster at work if you have one to can make that sandwich extra delicious.

Dinner: make sure you have plenty of variety to include things in your menu that could easily be used for your lunch the next day. Chicken could be made into a mouth watering salad the next day or a chicken wrap. Use your imagination and explore until you find a menu that works for you.

Chinese food is a tasty treat that can be made with ease. Buy dry noodles or rice and either make a mix or purchase a stir fry mix to add to your noodles or rice.

Baked beans and hot dogs can make a quick and cheap meal for one day in the week so that another day you can really treat yourself.

A variety of pastas with homemade or readymade sauces can provide a very filling meal. Macaroni cheese, pasta bake, paste and hot dogs, pasta and mince, pasta and tinned fish are all variations on the pasta meal.

Food from around the world could also be a meal plan you could consider,

Also think about one night a week having a vegetarian menu it may be a tasty treat for your palate and it may save you money.

Desserts are part of the meal that may just fill your belly. Crumbles and pies are easy to make or ready prepared packets are usually reasonably priced. Custard or (on special occasions) cream, clotted creams can dress up a very basic desert.

Snacks like cereal bars or flapjacks are very easy to make or readymade versions may still save you money and prevent you from expensive impulse purchases.

Biscuits, cookies or cakes are also very easy to make but readymade versions may still save you money and prevent you from expensive impulse purchases.

Remember small savings can make a real significant impact on your debt and moving towards being financially worry free.

Chapter 15: What about my debts? Are there letters I can write?

So you have debts and you are not sure what to do. Consider writing letters to the people you owe money to and let them know about your predicament. Use these as a guide or prompt to help you.

Remember to do your research as names of things vary in different parts of the World.

When you write your letter remember to include your address:

Your address

When you write your letter remember to include your creditor's address:

The address of the person you owe money too

When you write your letter remember to include the date:

Date

When you write your letter remember to include name of person writing to:

Dear Sir or Madame

When you write your letter remember to include relevant details like account number:

Reference/Case/Account number

Explain why and how you got into financial difficulties and include any relevant information or evidence:

This is a realistic amount given my circumstances

Please will you accept my offer of payment?

When you write your letter remember to include your plan of action and that you will keep them informed:

I will make a payment on

Thank you for your assistance

When you write your letter remember to state all the relevant details.

Remember to end your letter letting the person know you are awaiting their reply.

Chapter 16: How do we live the life of our dreams? What are the magic words you need to hear?

I hope that you are inspired to live the life of your dreams. I hope that you have heard the magic words you need to hear to stay focused and motivated. Before I depart, I want to share with you the story I told my friend.

Getting to a place where you are financially free is like doing a running race. The Big Fun 5k run was on Sunday and I successfully completed that in 34 minutes. But my success was not achieved on my own. What happened was quite unexpected.

During the race, I saw a man that was sweating profusely and looked like he was about to keel over. I stopped and asked him if he was okay. I engaged in conversation with him because I have been where he was. I had both empathy and understanding of his situation. I had to make a choice, but I knew what the right thing to do was because I also have been so out of breath and filled with terror because my body was not reacting the way it is supposed to, and my breathing was so erratic that I could just pass out.

So I made the decision to help this man. I stayed with this man during the remainder of the course and I shared my strategy with him. I told him let us run to the bench and then walk to the bins. I told him if you feel up to it we can keep going or stop when you need to. As we progressed through the course the man had more belief in my strategy and his breathing and pace continued to improve. This meant that we both completed the course and I did a personal best while helping another person.

In life there will always be someone who knows a strategy, or a secret to help us to achieve our goals. Slowing down to help someone out may seem like it is hindrance, but as in my case helping has always been beneficial to me. So I ask you, how can you help yourself by helping someone else? Can you share your tips for saving money or making extra money. Or your tips for getting your clothes at a discount, or an inexpensive time to go to a restaurant or cinema? There are so many things that you are an expert on, there are ways that we can help each other to be on the path to success. To being financially worry free. There must be something that you know could help a friend or family member.

We can all live the life of our dreams. We can all be with our partners planning our financial futures in a calm and rational way. We have to remember we don't have to be selfish to succeed. Someone else's downfall does not have to be the way to success. We must try to be the one person that is able to say I am going to live the life I want to live, a life that is financially worry free.

Let us be great role models for our friends, family, children and communities and offer that support or advice. Let us say the magic words to our self or to others so that they strive for success and live the life of their dreams.

I know that we can all live the life of our dreams, but we must know what those goals or dreams are. Write those lists and give each goal a time or deadline so that you are one step closer to achieving the life of your dreams.

So what are the magic words you need to hear? Stop thinking about what you want and get on and do something about it. Ask for help; find out more about how to achieve your goals. There are so many kind and generous people who will support you.

Find a mentor; find a friend that will remind you how amazing and wonderful you are. You are a winner and you will succeed.

Let me know how your challenges and successes work out. Remember you have to dream it and believe that you can take action. Know what you want to achieve and find out what you need to do it.

Good luck to us all and keep on believing in your dreams. Remember to hold on to that feeling of success and desire for change. The result will be that we will all be sharing how we are living the life we have been dreaming about.

If you need some help getting motivated check out my blog:

https://somespecialpeople.wordpress.com/

http://www.somespecialpeople.com/

https://somespecialpeople.wordpress.com/https://somespecialpeople.wordpress.com/

I really would love it if you let me know anything that would help to motivate you. I look forward to hearing about your success stories.

Chapter 17: Conclusion

I shall leave you with the wisdom of author Napoleon Hill; you need to remember you have a goal and that is to be financially worry free. You have a plan and you have told the one closest to you about your debts and you have expressed through words and actions what you desire and need to achieve. You are not going to let setbacks hold you back; you will continue to remain focused and driven towards your goal. You have formed an alliance with someone to help you to remain focused and you both have the same plan and purpose.

Persistence will carry you to your destination of being financially worry free.

Be clear and define exactly what you want.

"Whatever your mind can conceive and believe it can achieve." - Napoleon Hill

Sources used and so you may do more research

http://www.which.co.uk/money/credit-cards-and-loans/guides/how-to-deal-with-debt/10-ways-to-pay-off-your-debts/http://www.which.co.uk/money/credit-cards-and-loans/guides/how-to-deal-with-debt/10-ways-to-pay-off-your-debts/

http://www.moneysavingexpert.com/savings/pay-off-debtshttp://www.moneysavingexpert.com/savings/pay-off-debts

http://www.moneycrashers.com/pay-off-credit-card-debt-fast-plan/http://www.moneycrashers.com/pay-off-credit-card-debt-fast-plan/

http://www.resolver.co.uk/

http://www.somespecialpeople.com/

https://somespecialpeople.wordpress.com/

Cally Finsbury

Cally Finsbury was born and raised in London where the diverse community and surroundings were her playground. Long winters and wonderful summers cultivated her love of books.

As a child, she was blessed with a vivid imagination. Her young friends begged for the stories she spun. She used her imagination to avoid boredom and create enjoyment.

From her fleeting glimpse of childhood came adulthood with a variety of careers and worldwide travel.

The business world was explored, then marriage and motherhood, all building blocks for a storyteller to emerge as a novelist.

Her diverse writing skills even extend to romance and how to books.

Author Cally Finsbury is one busy writer. In addition to her children novels, she also writes with her three sons under the pen name Mr Cally Finsbury.

Cally and her family want to spread awareness of special needs and encourage people to be motivated to live the life of their dreams.

http://www.resolver.co.uk/

http://www.resolver.co.uk/

http://www.resolver.co.uk/